This is How I Roll

Jim Hardy

ISBN 978-1-0980-7484-5 (paperback)
ISBN 978-1-0980-7586-6 (hardcover)
ISBN 978-1-0980-7485-2 (digital)

Christian Faith Publishing, Inc.
832 Park Avenue
Meadville, PA 16335
www.christianfaithpublishing.com

Printed in the United States of America

Opening

Well, I guess to go back and begin where life changed for me would be a good place to start. This is where I realized there's something going on with this world, something bigger than anyone, and something no man can understand. Maybe that's what God intended—a world not to understand but to just have faith. I've had so many times I thought I could do life on my own only to find out I needed Him in everything.

My story began on a cool overcast fall morning. I awoke like any other fall day in college, thinking of enjoying college life. On this morning, I had time before my first class to drive up to my family land to hunt a few hours before coming back to school. I met up with my friend Bryant, whom I met in college, to go hunting. We arrived to my family's land just before daylight. I walked to my hunting area and climbed up into a tree to hunt. The next thing I remembered was waking up on the ground and looking up at the tree I was just sitting in. I laid there not sure what had happened but also noticed one ray of sunshine shining through the clouds straight at me on this cloudy morning. What this meant, I wasn't sure. What I did know was that I was unable to get up when I tried to move. At this point, thoughts began to run through my mind. *Do I yell for help? Do I try to get up again? Could I be dreaming some crazy dream?* The most calming feeling came over me like when you know you're protected, and nothing can get to you. It was as if someone said, *Hey, I am here with you; don't worry.* So I rested there on that ground knowing everything was going to be all right. Thankfully and unbeknownst to me, Bryant, my friend, had already sensed something had gone wrong with me. He later shared with me that an uneasy feeling came over him and that was when he decided to climb down and headed toward me. While heading my way, he began yelling my name, and he recalled becoming more frantic when I did not respond. God definitely spoke to Bryant that day. As Bryant headed out to find help, the first person he saw was a pastor in his yard. The pastor was able to seek help and led emergency personnel into the woods. The next thing I remembered was seeing a large group of people including my grandfather and Bryant helping to load me onto a board. They carried me through the woods and into an ambulance.

We headed to the local hospital. I entered the emergency room where a nurse began to cut off my camouflage clothes. Even through all of the chaos and fear, all I could think about was the fact that she was cutting off my brand new camouflage that I had worked so hard all summer to save up and buy. When the doctor entered, he saw the severity of my injuries to my body and said, "We need to get him to a larger hospital for surgery now." I heard his words but still had a calm feeling. Something just would not let me feel any pain. During the trip to the larger hospital, I fell asleep. I woke up in the larger hospital and found out from my nurse that I had surgery to repair my broken back, broken ribs, collapsed lung, fractured hip, and internal bleeding. Still, hearing this list of bad news, I kept a calm feeling like someone was there with me. The nurse told me I was not out of trouble yet. I asked her why. She gave me the news that my body was having trouble stabilizing. She said that my body was rejecting salt and that each day here, my sodium levels have continued to drop. She let me know that I could die if my levels got too low. The doctors came in and told me that for several days, anything I wanted to eat would have to be covered in salt and that I could not have water. If I was thirsty, I had to call a nurse and have a sponge with water put in my mouth for a few seconds. This went on for many days. Each morning, my sodium numbers continued to decrease.

Through the door of my room each morning, I could hear the doctors talk and review my notes from the past several days' levels. One morning, I heard one of them say what nobody wanted to hear.

"I've tried all I know to do and still no changes. If he goes a couple more days like this, he won't make it."

Another doctor responded, "I guess we're just going to have to get lucky with this one."

My heart fell to the floor!

At that point, I knew I needed to speak to an old friend, one my grandmother had introduced me to on Sundays many years ago. When I would spend the weekend with my grandparents, they would take me to church. Getting me there was not the easiest thing. See, when I was little, I loved the outdoors more than anything on earth. I wanted to be outside running in the woods, fishing in my grandfather's pond, and playing in the wide open fields. The best place I could find to do that was on my grandparents' farm. Every day that I did not have school and every weekend, I wanted to be at their house enjoying the outdoors. Every Sunday morning, it did not matter what I was doing, my grandmother always said, "Time for church." I did not understand why I had to go because they went to a small church, and for many Sundays, I sat in a Sunday school class all alone. After Sunday school, I would sit with my grandparents and watch their pastor turn all kinds of colors yelling and telling a crowd about some man that could change their lives. I learned about this man that could fix anything. He was a man so big that He watches over the whole world. I heard stories for years about people at their church who asked for help and got it. I always thought, *I don't need help. I can handle anything alone.* When I heard the words of the doctors loud and clear, I knew there was only one person to ask for help. I went to Him that night in my hospital bed. I prayed to Him, "Lord, if this is my time, I understand. If this is the way you want me to leave this world, I don't understand, but it's okay. Lord, if this is not my time, give me a sign, and show me the man that many people speak of but never see. I will rest my head tonight knowing that whatever happens is in your hands." Then just like the day of my accident, I got a calming feeling, almost like I knew everything would be okay. The next thing I remember was waking up to a nurse informing me that I was stable, and they were moving me from the

ICU to a regular room. It was at that moment that I knew all that God wanted was for me to believe, and everything would be okay.

It is not always clear what I need to do, and it's also not easy dealing with life's day-to-day challenges, but it sure does help to have an old friend by your side on the road.

Within a few weeks, I was healthy enough to leave the hospital and head home. Now my new life was about to begin: taking on what life had in store for me in my new rolling chair. Knowing that I had a copilot on my flight through this upcoming life challenge of going through life in a wheelchair sure made me feel good.

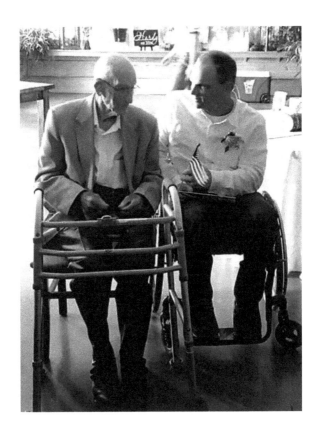

Rolling in the Real World

As I entered into this new way of life and a new chapter within my life, many questions, concerns, and thoughts consumed me about how I will take on this big world from a wheelchair. I started to think about the new lens I must look through to view the world—sitting low, seeing people at their waist, and wheeling everywhere I go. I came home from the hospital knowing I only had two classes left to get my college degree, something no one in my family has ever accomplished. I wanted this degree so badly. I had worked so many years studying long nights and working hard to finish. I knew I had to go back to school and finish what I started. Little did I know what things I would face in my new world with four wheels guiding my every move and taking me down every path life led me. Every choice I made from visiting other friends to shopping downtown, eating out, dates, these four wheels gave me the chance to be like everybody else, enjoying a normal life every day.

Most people never stop and think of the view from a wheelchair or even realize the road bumps we face. To roll around everywhere you go is definitely a challenge and a unique view of life. I have seen many people look at me, turn around, and walk the other way. People have pointed and talked. I have even heard a mother tell her children, "Don't get around him…he's crippled." Instead of doing these things, try to see what you can do to help that person get where they want to go. My hope is, by writing this book, people will see the person, not the wheelchair. Life is always going to be full of bumps, but you can sure help smoothen the ride with just a little help. Do not ever give up on a person with a disability because you could have the ability they are looking for—the ability to add things to their life that no one else can. Let's lift each other up. You may find out that the person in the wheelchair can teach you way more than you can ever teach them.

Back to my story. This is what I saw entering the new college of life in a chair, rolling in the real world. Let's begin with a daily issue: ramps. The ramps were made to give me a place to go up on curbs and then into a store or building. Most people never notice these ramps. At gas stations and other businesses, there's usually only one ramp. I have seen many people, including police officers, park right in front of the ramp resulting in me having no way to get into the business.

The next issue is restroom accessibility. Many restrooms have a wide enough door to get into but then fall way short once inside. The stalls are not big enough for a chair, and most sinks are not high enough to get a chair under. I have to reach for soap and paper towels. I never wanted to complain to anyone; I would just always find a way to overcome the problem on my own.

I experienced some stores that were not very accessible, narrowing aisles, things blocking rolling paths, but I have found that most stores would help me get whatever I need if asked. Also, a plus is that the more I go to a store, the more they worked hard to fix their store for me and others like me. So by getting out of my home and doing everyday things, I felt like I was helping others that came after me.

Lastly, some other challenges are sidewalks and parking lots. Sidewalks are a big one because I have spent a lot of my travel time at college using sidewalks to get me where I needed to go. Older cities have old, cracked, and several unlevelled places within their sidewalks. What I had not thought of just yet was that just a half inch difference could mean my chair tipping to one side and rolling me onto the concrete. Let me tell you from experience: concrete hurts when you fall on it. I once had a problem with a sidewalk in town. I went to the management and asked about fixing the problem, not complaining. They fixed the issue quickly and thanked me for making them aware of the issue because they had not seen it from the view of someone in a wheelchair. To help you see the view I was talking about, I was reminded of a story that happened at my apartment in college.

One day, I went to the grocery store. I crawled out of bed, got a shower, crawled back in bed, and put my clothes on. Next, I got my wallet, medical supplies, and headed out the door to my truck. Once I got across the parking lot to my truck, I realized I had forgotten my keys, so I wheeled back to the apartment to find the apartment door locked. I remembered the sliding patio door was open, so I had to go under the apartment building, slightly uphill on as flat ground as I could find through landscape bushes along the building's edge. As I got close to the back of the apartment building, I got my wheels stuck in the soft dirt around the landscape bushes. Frustrated but left with no other choice, I got out of my chair onto the ground and crawled to my patio door that was open. Suddenly it hit me, I needed my chair to be able to get around inside, but it was still in the bushes. I crawled back to my chair and dragged it, by hand, through the bushes. I would crawl a few feet and drag the chair a few feet. Close to 150 feet later, I was back to my patio. I dragged the chair inside and was able to climb back into it. After all of this, I was worn out. Going to the grocery store was just going to have to wait. All of this could have been avoided had I not forgotten my keys or had a plan for that situation. Plus, here's another hard lesson I learned from getting in and out of my truck. I once got out of my truck and sat down on the brake for the wheels and cut the back of my leg open, and I was bleeding everywhere. That metal sticking up cut you if you missed that seat cushion when landing in the chair, and it was not fun. That seemed to be the key to this whole new life in a wheelchair: the view. I had to start viewing every place I would go with new eyes—eyes focused on my needs for trips plus doors, ramps, and sidewalks, even the way I would get in my chair before I would ever go out because I could waste a lot of time and physical energy going nowhere.

For me, when I roll through the real world each and every day, I am reminded of a story that my Sunday school teacher talked about from the Bible. A boy named David wanted to take on a mighty Philistine named Goliath. This Goliath had killed many big and strong men, but David, being only a boy, had to have the courage to step out and fight this superhuman-like man. Just by stepping out, God gave him superhuman-like strength, and he defended himself against Goliath with just one small stone. I tell you this story for one reason: I get my strength and courage every day knowing that God can give me the strength to push through any obstacle the real world might put in front of me along my path in life. If I could come up with the courage to roll out, then He always put someone or something in my path to help me reach my goal. Sometimes things felt like that story of David and Goliath: me against the world, but God has always provided a way for me.

Now, after experiencing college life and the daily struggles traveling to and from class, rolling around college town, going on dates, and finishing my last two classes, I had learned what was out in the real world in daily life. I learned many lessons during my first year in a chair. The view is starting to become clear of what my new world would be like. Rolling each and every day is not easy knowing what could be ahead, but with faith, I was ready for it. With a little thought about what I want to do and what it will take to get me there, anything is possible.

Trying New Things

At this point in the book, I've told you about how I got into a chair and my new view on life, but what I think you need to know is that there is still a lot more to me. I enjoyed doing a lot of different things in my spare time before my injury, so after my injury, I still had the same desires in my heart. I just was not sure if I could do the same things.

Being in a wheelchair may seem to be a handicap, but I think it is what you make of it or do not make of it that is the handicap. I try not to limit myself on what I can do. Things that enter my heart and I have a true passion for, I try them and have faith that God will work them out for me. Just months after leaving the hospital, one thing I found, by trying new things, was painting. I was asked by a good friend to try painting because they knew I liked to draw in my spare time. So I decided that it could not hurt anything to try. My first few paintings looked really rough, given I had never painted before. However after several tries, I got the hang of it. I even had someone ask if they could buy my painting! Wait, what? Yes, it blew me away too! So after one small painting sold, that gave me the motivation to keep going. Soon, without realizing it, I had sold over two hundred paintings. Not too bad for somebody that just decided to try something new. I also realized painting was relaxing, fun, and loved by people of all walks of life. No, I was not a world-famous painter, but maybe that was God's plan. I was only supposed to paint to relax from everyday life, have fun, and brighten a few peoples' day and learn what He was teaching through painting. I had been to a lot of art shows, met many kind, sweet, and wonderful people and made a few lifelong friends. God knew I needed painting for that chapter of my life. I still paint to this day for fun, relaxation, and when someone calls and wants to buy a painting.

That led me to my next adventure. Someone I met, when selling paintings, asked me to come speak at their church. For most, it is their greatest fear: sitting in a room full of people and wondering what they are thinking of you. I promise, it was no different when I was first asked to do it. I had to stop and think for a minute. Here is God giving me another chance to step out and do something I have never done. Then it was placed on my heart: *what if someone needs to hear my story to help them with something they are going through?* I figured if I did not try, then I could be missing out on a chance to help someone. I also decided to pray and let God take care of me while I spoke. It turned out great! I began to speak and had a calming feeling around me the whole time. I really enjoyed telling other people about my story, hearing their stories, and how they needed to hear what I had to say. That night, I also got asked to speak again to a youth group. As they say, the rest is crazy! I have since spoken hundreds of times to churches, colleges, high schools, sports teams, business leadership groups for team building, and many other groups. Thinking back to all of those speeches that I have done, most people would say the most memorable was speaking to a major college team before they played their rival and won! For me, it was speaking to a group of adult men, telling them my story and wondering if I was connecting to them or even making sense to them. My answer soon came as I neared the end of my speech. I looked around the room to see tears coming from several men. When I was done and went to leave, I heard a man behind me say, "Hey, sir, thank you." It was a man with tears in his eyes.

He said, "I needed that, sir. You made me realize that life's been rough, but I've still got a chance to do some good things."

I drove home that night realizing that if I had not listened to God and not taken the offer to speak, I would have missed my chance to help someone. Speaking to a crowd or one person is not a lot different but just in your mind. We focus on the fear of what people think of us instead of focusing on what you say could change someone's life. Even if you only share your story with one person, that could be the key to unlocking their whole world. I try every day to listen to what I get told by God, but as humans, we fight what God says to do, but it always works out that His way is the best.

Pawsitively Fun

I was at a speaking event one time and saw a blind man with a dog. That got me thinking. I like dogs and thought it would be good to have a friend to ride with me and help me around the house. That night, I was watching TV and saw a man training Labrador retrievers to fetch, swim, and basic obedience. That moment changed my life. I felt, in my heart, that I wanted a dog and that I needed to go see that man. His name was Mr. Woody. When I called him, we spoke at least an hour on the phone. He was so nice and told me to come look at his pups and pick one out. Well, that's where this chapter of my life gets interesting. Mr. Woody's wife placed a whole litter of puppies on the ground, away from my wheelchair, for me to see which one I liked. As I watched the whole litter play with each other on the ground, one puppy left the group and crawled to my chair and put his head on my foot. In his own special way, he picked me. I picked him up; he licked my face, and from then on, we were connected. I named him Champ. It was one of those moments when you know everything is going to be all right.

Mr. Woody and I talked about him training Champ for me. He said to take him home until he was six months old and bring him back for training. He told me that from six weeks to six months old, things learned by Champ about me would stick with him for life. I gave him the name Champ because his dad was a world field trial retrieving champion. He and I shared a bond so special that nothing else could replace it. It was something so unique that you know God played a role in lining it all up. Those first five months went fast, and I took Champ back for training. It was hard leaving him there for three whole months. I worried how he was doing at school. Was he warm? Was he hungry? Was he happy? Three months went by fast, and I found myself speeding to get him home. When I got there, I found that Champ had become an amazing dog. He could now swim all the way across a lake and bring a plastic duck back. He could run into a big field and find anything you could hide. One cool thing he learned was to pick up anything that I dropped like my keys, wallet, or phone. Mr. Woody was so smart. He went to a thrift store and bought a wheelchair to train him. The first dog he had ever trained from a wheelchair, in forty years of working with dogs, was for me.

I enjoyed my years with my buddy. We went fishing, hunting, speaking, and pretty much did everything together. One funny story about him, Champ enjoyed shopping. I would take him to the store to let him pick out anything he wanted. Believe it or not, he could pull something off the shelf himself, hold it in his mouth until we got to the register, and put it on the checkout counter by himself. Sometimes he would look around for a while then pick a toy. Other times, he wanted dog treats. Most times, he had a small crowd watching him, amazed at what he just did. I have to say, it was pretty cool to live with a celebrity! Champ and I won several ribbons for field trial competitions and went on some cool hunting trips together. One thing I can say about champ is he never met a person he didn't like. I loved that dog and everything about him. Not only did he make life in a wheelchair easier, he made other people and kids that played with him happy.

I remember one time, a child came to an event I was at, but he was shy and didn't want to talk to anyone. He even went to his room to get away from everyone else. Champ was with me, and he left my side and went to this kid's room and got in bed with him and started playing and licking him. Soon, all we could hear from that room was laughing. The little boy and champ had made friends. The rest of the weekend, the little boy was no longer shy as long as champ was with him. What a special thing God did when he made dogs. I once heard it said, "Give a dog your heart, and he'll give you his." Champ did not care what I had, who my friends were, or even what was going on in the world. In his mind, he was at peace playing or resting with me. I was at peace knowing he loved me no matter what I was going through. How many people can we say that about? In this ever-changing wheelchair life, I felt happy to have met and been loved by Champ.

Catching My Heart

While I was enjoying life with Champ, something still burned in my heart each day. I still had this strong passion to chase my dreams of fishing. This passion has been part of me since I was a little boy growing up. I was introduced to fishing by my grandfathers as a small child. That was where this passion got into my soul.

Fishing is such a diverse activity that it can be done by the smallest of children and can be so complex that grown adults chase fish from coast to coast. Fishing allows everyone to reach a wide range of emotions that no other sport can. Fishing can be relaxing and peaceful fun for the whole family. It is also so competitive that once a year, a tournament is held for one million dollars that goes to the best fisherman in the world. Fishing is also the only sport that, most of the time, you cannot see your opponent. This sport can even feed your family.

I was once asked what fishing means to me. It means thousands of memories from childhood: learning to fish with my grandfathers and my father, and I spent some of the greatest days of my young childhood sitting on a pond bank with my dad and grandfathers. I got to hear lots of stories from their past and learn so many life lessons from them. I now teach kids to fish just like they taught me. Fishing has allowed me to see places and moments in time that cannot be put into words.

See, on the water, you learn that every day is a new day, just like life—a new day learning what the fish will bite that day and a new day of weather. No two days are alike. See, fishing is kind of like life—you throw a lure in the water hoping to get a fish to bite. While you wait for that bite, you start thinking how exciting that moment is going to be when you reel in that big fish. Life seems to be the same way. We throw our hopes and dreams out there with the hopes we catch our dreams and reel in a great life. But there is a story in the Bible God talks about these fishermen that fished their way all day and did not catch a thing, then God said, "Cast your nets to the other side of the boat." And they caught their nets full. I have learned this same lesson when I do life my way. I did not catch much, but when I let Him guide me, I caught a lot. I have sat in my boat and fished all day with snow falling on me. I have sat through high winds, rain, breathtaking heat, and bone-chilling cold, but I always wanted to go back and learn more.

My first tournament I ever fished alone was seventeen degrees with ice on the deck of my boat. Each time I reeled my reel, water coming in on the line was freezing as it hit the deck of the boat. I really have to love something to do it in that kind of weather, plus the pain from injuries. My boat seat was once so hot in summer that I burned a hole on the bottom of my butt and had to lie in bed for three B months just to heal it. Let me tell you: it was not easy crawling around on a boat to do what I love.

God has put me in some beautiful places while sitting on the front of a boat, but after thousands of hours on the water, I started to see another picture that my GPS was trying to show me. While riding to a fishing tournament, I saw my GPS navigation on my dash. My GPS helps me find the places I am looking to go on the lake and traveling. I thought, *What is GPS? Was it God's Placement System?* I have been through a lot of tough times over the years, but I have realized God always placed the right people in my path and placed me in the place I needed to be if I let him. I am reminded of one story where I had a big fishing tournament to attend and something happened, health wise, to cause me not to go practice for the tournament, but I got better by the end of the week. I decided by not practicing that I would not go to the fishing tournament. Toward the end of that week, I was asked to go to a fishing event for children with disabilities. I went, and my life was changed forever. While at this event, I got to meet and fish with one child that touched my life. It was a little boy with the biggest smile on his face that I had ever seen. He had a nurse with him twenty-four hours a day because he had so many medical issues. He was in a wheelchair, could not move his legs or arms, and could barely move his fingers. We were fishing in a small pond.

I got the fishing pole ready with bait and told the little boy, "Okay, here's the pole. Throw the bait in the water to catch a fish."

His nurse said, "Oh, he can't do that. You just have to catch fish and let him see it."

He had been at this event for the past three years, and his fishing helper always caught a fish and let him see it. Well, I thought there had to be a way for him to throw the pole and catch a fish with some help. I asked her to let me work with him to help him throw the pole. I placed the pole in his hand, and we threw it together in the water. Then as quick as the bait hit the water, a fish had it pulling on the line. I left the pole in his hand, and then I held his other hand, and we reeled the fish in. With each turn of the reel, the fish got closer, and a smile started to form on his face. We soon had the fish out of the water, and I held it up to let him see what he had caught. As he and I celebrated his catch, his nurse leaned over to say thank you.

She then said, "I need to tell you something. I know you can see the hose going from his back to nose, but what you don't know is that his health has gotten worse where he needs oxygen every few minutes to help him breathe." She told me that this fishing trip was possibly his last because of his health. Then someone told me that I was a true blessing because I showed him that he could do more than he and everyone else thought he could. For him to catch a fish, with help, was amazing. After seeing me in a wheelchair teach someone else in a wheelchair to do something that they thought they could not was teaching them. She said that maybe she could do more than even she thought she could to help this little boy and others and thanked me for the help.

Driving home, I realized that God was placing me where I needed to be, not where I wanted to be. I could have been in a completely different place that day. He taught me that I do matter in this world, and I can help others by just being myself. Fishing also lead me to fish with a group called the Paralyzed Veterans of America, PVA. Both my grandfathers were veterans in the Air Force and the Navy, and my father was in the Army National Guard. I saw and heard what serving their country meant to them. So I definitely wanted to be part of such an amazing group helping veterans fish. I enjoyed traveling the country and meeting some amazing men that served our country with their lives to make sure we could enjoy activities like fishing. I fished in fishing tournaments in Washington, Illinois, Texas, Florida, Georgia, Tennessee, South Carolina, Alabama, and many other states.

Here's one funny story while fishing a tournament in Illinois. I was going to practice fishing one day and put my boat in the water. I realized I had left my motor holder on that stops the motor from bouncing while driving the boat down the road on a trailer. When the boat enters the water, this tool needs to be off the motor for it to work right in the water. I hurried to crawl to the back of the boat to get it off, and in the process of crawling on the boat carpet, it pulled my shorts and underwear to my ankles. There I laid in my birthday suit in a state park in Illinois totally by accident but very funny. I got my shorts back up, but I bet I laughed about it for an hour after that. I enjoyed their fishing trial so much. I did well enough fishing a season with them to make their end-of-the-year championship. It was in Arkansas where I finished second in the nation among disabled anglers. While there, I realized how blessed I was just to be fishing in Arkansas. I won second place for $2,500. I decided to donate all of the money to the American Red Cross. They seem to help a lot of people in their time of need. I figured God blessed me with a good tournament finish so I could bless others too.

After that, fishing led me to fishing weekend series style tournaments made for local fishermen to try to compete against the best in your home state. I loved the trail, cashed several checks, and almost won two tournaments with a few crazy stories. One of which I had fished all day and caught some nice fish. About one hour before the tournament was over, I caught a big fish and had to cull out my smallest fish of five as the rules say. My co-angler helped me, but he laid all of my fish in the floor of my boat. He accidentally threw out my small and biggest fish causing me to lose the tournament. With my biggest fish, I would have won the tournament. It was a total accident, but I learned a lesson: always enjoy the day, the moment, and the blessings you have. I had enough big fish to win the tournament, but to no fault of mine, I lost it. Maybe the person that won that day needed the money really bad, and God blessed him.

I once was practicing for a tournament and had to use the restroom bad. I was in the middle of the lake. As you know, being in a wheelchair, I can't jump off the boat into the woods like most people. I had to take off my shirt, use the restroom into it, and throw it in the trash. I spent the rest of the day shirtless and sunburned. Not a funny story I know, but that is wheelchair life. After a few years of that series of tournaments, I decided to move on and upward. I tried fishing the open style tournaments against professional anglers. I took two years, traveled the country, and fished against the best anglers in the world. I learned really fast, just why they are the best in the world. I had a lot of fun traveling the roads with two of the world's best fisherman: Greg Vinson and Mark Menendez; they stayed in some cool places and some pretty rough ones too. I have got to say, what you see on TV is not half of what it takes to be a professional angler.

One funny and painful story for you. I caught a fish once on a top-water lure that has nine hooks on it. As I swung the fish into the boat, it landed on my leg placing six of those hooks into my leg and a fighting fish on the others. As it flopped, it ripped my skin leaving blood everywhere. I finally got the fish stopped from flopping, unhooked it from the lure, then slowly removed each hook from my leg. I had to wrap my leg with a shirt and continue fishing because tournaments do not stop just because an angler is injured. So I stuck it out, pain and all, until the end of the day, but hard work does pay off. I was able to travel to Lake Santee Cooper and cash a check with many people in my life saying I would never do it. I became the first disabled angler ever to cash a check as a professional. Since then, others have come along and cashed checks, but to be the first meant something to me because I did not come to win money. I just came to fish because I love fishing. I think God wanted others to see what He could do through me.

In tournament fishing, you have got guys that get to ride with me as their boat captain. One fisherman found out he got me and got upset. I even heard him say, "I got the guy in the wheelchair. Just my luck!" On the day before, I had figured out what the fish liked to bite and was ready for the tournament. The next day, during the tournament, no matter where I went on the lake, I caught fish. My co-angler that just the night before did not want to ride in my boat started asking questions. He wanted to know how I was catching all of those fish, what kind of lures were I using, could he try one. So just like that, he no longer saw my chair. He saw a person that could help him catch fish. By the end of the day, you would have thought I was the greatest fisherman in the world. He talked so much; I could not make him stop. We got back to the boat ramp, and he started telling all of his friends about me, then they wanted to know how I learned to catch fish like that. After weighing my fish, I finished high enough in that tournament that I got a check. I drove home thanking God for the blessings the whole way. I was not sure what kind of sign that was, but I really felt good knowing that if I did my best, He would do the rest.

One thing every fisherman wants to do is have their name on a lure. I was no different. I always wanted to do something to give back to fishing and help others catch fish. My plan started with drawings and gluing other lures together to see what I could make. I found out it was tougher than it looked. I tried many ideas and went through many drafts. I finally came up with a good-looking lure, but I had to figure out how to make it in a mold where it could be mass-produced. God stepped in again and put Braxton, a lure designer, in my path. He helped me finalize the details, and the Hardytack Craw was born. I told him that I did not want any profit from the lure. All I wanted was to help fishermen to catch fish and for him to help some special kids that I know. My lure was produced and sold in all major fishing stores in the country even in South Africa and Japan. It was not about the money. It was about helping others enjoy the outdoors. Even all the money I won in fishing tournaments over the years, I gave it to different charities. I figured I was blessed by God just to be healthy enough to fish, so why couldn't I help others with my blessings from God?

After traveling around helping sell fishing lures for a few years, I felt led to leave tournament fishing behind. So now, I do only special kids fishing events to help other kids learn to fish. I even have a seven-acre lake in my front yard where hundreds of kids have come here for events and caught their first fish. My next chapter of life was my love for football. See, when I was hurt, I was working with a college football team as a student assistant. I always wanted to coach football. That was my dream after college, but when the injury happened, I kind of set football aside. I had never seen any coaches in wheelchairs before.

The Football Story

Jim Hardy leads Victory Christian to fourth state title in 6 years

Growing up, I was not ever good at football, but I always wanted to play. My high school years, I struggled to find a spot on my big high school team to start. I taught myself how to punt because I realized I wasn't the fastest, strongest, or best tackler on the team. So kicking and punting was the best spot for me if I was going to find a way onto the field to play. I worked hard each year trying to get better each season. I would take our school's bag of footballs and go kick during the summer, all by myself in one-hundred-degree heat, in hopes to strengthen my leg and get better at kicking and punting. I ended up being the school's all-time best punter my senior year in a vote held by a local sports show. All my hard work had paid off for my final year to play high school football. I had in one night punts of eighty-four and seventy yards. That's not too bad on a one-hundred-yard field. After high school, I went off to college and knew I still loved football and wanted to be a part of a team somewhere. I decided to attend a university where I made friends with some players on the team and started punting footballs with them during the summer for the punt returners to practice. One day, I got noticed by the special team's coach, and he offered for me to walk on because I was good enough to play college football. I told him I could not afford to walk on because I needed a job to pay for school and that would not leave me time to attend practice and meetings. I ended up taking an offer to be a student assistant on the university team and that gave me a way to still be involved with football. I enjoyed four years of helping the college team. We traveled to some beautiful college stadiums and saw some of the world's greatest football players play the game they love. I love the game and the amazing way the game teaches so many great things to young men. One thing I saw was it puts young men from all walks of life in a huddle and teaches them to work together.

After college was over, I got asked by a good friend to help him coach his high school team one season. I really enjoyed that season and realized I knew I was where God wanted me to be. Even though that team only won one game all season, I really saw their ability and love for the game. The next season, I was asked to be the team's head coach and took it as a huge honor to even be asked. I researched the school to find out they had never had a winning season in school history and usually got beat pretty badly in games. My first thought, as a coach, was that I wanted to focus on the players having a positive attitude, putting forth their best effort, and knowing the details of the game. My first season, our team went undefeated and won the state championship. That season was something pretty special: to see kids that didn't think they could win start winning. It was also motivating for me.

I heard a coach from the other team at our first game of that season said, "That sure is sweet they let him coach." Then other comments to follow, "How is he gonna coach from a wheelchair?" We won that game 56–0. God taught me a lot about myself that season and our chance to help others with the resources he gave us. I knew football, and they had the heart and talent to play the game. When we worked together, good things happened. We also added an extra team member every year—a special kid to help our boys see life's not just about football. It was amazing to see our young men go to their extra teammate and want to score for them. Those young men set the table for all the years of winning to come.

A pretty cool story, one year, our team won a championship game when it came down to half of a second…yes, a half second! See, we had twelve seconds remaining before the third downplay. I called a running play, and our running back ran right, and the defense was there, then he ran back left, and the defense was there again. After all of his running backward, I yelled. "Lay down." He did, and they touched him. The clock had 0.6 seconds on it. We got one more play, and I prayed and asked God to give "the" play! Well He did just that; we ran it and won the state championship with no time left on the clock.

I have some amazing stories over the years from our boys overcoming the odds and winning. In my six years as head coach, we went to the state championship game all six years and ended up winning the state championship four years plus we're runners-up the other two years. We also received a resolution honoring our team for two straight prefect seasons from the senate of the State of Alabama. That's just one of many awards our boys earned with their four state titles. Another amazing blessing was my final season as head coach. We were undefeated and unscored on. We did not give up a single point the entire season. There was no doubt that God put the right kids, right families and everything we needed together in order to compete at such a high level. Winning games are hard enough, but to see these kids focus and prepare to the level not to give up any points says a lot about these kids' will to win. It's something pretty special to see young men put in the hard work, and it all pay off for championships! Watching the love for each other in their eyes after a championship, that's what it's all about. I used to pray before games, "God, give me the ability to call good plays and allow my boys to play well and stay safe from injury, and let us all honor your name."

I viewed the field from a wheelchair with some fear of getting run into on the sideline, but at the same time, I saw myself as having the greatest seat in the house. One statement I always told my boys, once you cross that line, I'm not going with you, so you better be ready. Life of a coach in a wheelchair is not easy: intense arm pain, severe shoulder pain, rolling that long and wide field. Got to follow the players every play of the game and then go all the way to the locker room at halftime and all the way back to the sideline after, even practicing in one-hundred-degree summertime heat. Then being so exhausted that I would pass out as soon as I got home, sleep all night, and do it again the next day. I covered a lot of miles rolling in a game and possibly one hundred miles in a season. That is a lot of work from a chair.

I love each boy I coached so much that I wrote their names in my Bible so when I opened it each time, it reminded me to pray for them and their safety through their travels in life. I toughed it out each season and every game to make sure I did my part to help my boys have a chance to win. I am just a part of a team. It takes everybody working together to win championships. My boys were never going to see me quit. I asked them for all they had every Friday night, and I wasn't going to give them any less than my all! I even gave my pay back to the school. In six years of being a head coach, I never received a dime. I even bought uniforms, cleats, clothes, and equipment for the team out of my own pocket. Because I don't have a son and I thought of each of those boys as my own son, and I would want my own son to have the best and play his best. Coaching has never been about the money to me; it was about helping young boys grow into young men.

Planted

Along with coaching, I love planting things like trees, vegetables, and flowers for my wife, daughter, and the wildlife on our land. I have always enjoyed growing plants while helping both of my grandfathers and father in their gardens when I was younger. God has planted me in a lot of places in my life and taught me a lot through planting things on my land. This chapter of my life takes me back to my childhood.

I grew up around family that loved to garden. They grew vegetables of all kinds. Granddad used to say, "Ain't nothing like fresh homegrown vegetables." He was right. The taste is amazing, the sweetness straight off the plant. The older I get, I have started to realize that God has taught me so many lessons through growing plants of all kinds. I have recently started planting trees of all kinds on my property. A man starts to see clearly once he understands the trees he plants will provide shade and fruit to future generations. That future generations many not know the man that planted the tree they sit under, but that's okay because maybe that's part of God's plan. Some of our greatest blessings were planted by people we never know. One thing about a tree is that you cannot rush its growth. The best trees grow slow, big, and strong. Fruit trees and oak trees sometimes take years to see their fruit, nuts, and all their hard work of growth, but when you do, it is amazing to see. Sometimes God has plans to plant us in areas during different times in our life just to produce our fruit later. I have seen so many times that God had a plan that I was planted in areas that didn't make sense at the time. In so many areas of my life, it took years to produce fruit because I needed to go through several things to grow in God's Word and see that He had a plan the whole time.

One plant I love growing is watermelon, and I enjoy its sweet and juicy taste. I was told my mother craved watermelon when I was in her belly. So I guess watermelons are in my blood. My favorite varieties of melons take 90–100 days to make fruit. I think God shows us through plants some sweet things we want can take time, but it all begins when we stick that seed in the ground and must have faith it will grow out of the ground. See the soil must be rich with nutrients and fertilizer for your seed to have a chance to grow. God taught me that life is the same way. If you hang out with bad people, you won't grow, so plant yourself and your seeds in good soil. Then we see it pop-up in a few days, but then again we must have faith for ninety more days that it will produce fruit. Faith is a tough thing sometimes to wait on God. Sometimes we must wait in stages and show God our faith in the first stage to be able to get to where he shows us our fruit. If you're willing to plant a seed in your life, it doesn't have to be a plant; it could be work, a project, or someone else's life. Just give your best, and you'll see the fruits of your labor with faith.

I started with the idea to plant one or two oak trees on my land for the deer to have acorns; then that became ten different varieties of oaks then that became fifty oak trees. The thought was that I wanted to give all God's wildlife any kind of acorn they could ever want. The idea grew into fruit trees for the wildlife. Before I knew it, I planted close to a hundred and fifty oak and fruit trees. What a way to leave something behind, after I am gone, for the wildlife and for my family to eat. You too can plant seeds in the ground or in your life, and you'll help others for years to come. A plant must push through the dirt to prove itself. We have to push ourselves through the dirt in this world in order to grow.

One day, I was thanking God for all He had given me. He taught me…He was teaching me through planting that we're like a tree; when planted in the right soil, we'll grow for many years to come producing fruit for many generations. Plant yourself in good soil…good friends, and a good network of good, godly people, and you will produce God's plan for many generations to come.

OFF

This is one of my favorite areas of my life and journey through this world. I always had a passion for helping people, especially children. After my injury, I became much more aware of a specific group that wasn't provided with the same outdoor opportunities as I was all my life. See, it is not the duration of your life, it is your donation to it. When a person gives back some of what they have to help others, they become part of a special group of people—the group that is able to see how it feels to change someone's life. Try doing small acts of kindness helping others with their goals. It may seem small, but you will see that you can give something small that makes a big difference in someone's dreams. One of the smallest things I had ever done that made the biggest difference was on a hunting weekend with disabled children. I help run hunting camps for special children. During this weekend, we teach archery, shooting, and general hunting skills to special children who have always wanted to learn about the outdoors but have never had someone to help them. I formed a group of my friends to help teach these children. One of my big things each year is that I ask each child, If I could do one thing to make this weekend the greatest weekend of your life, what would it be?

I heard this little voice say, "I got one!"

It was a little eleven-year-old boy who said that he knew what he wanted.

I said, "Okay, tell me."

In the back of my mind, I was thinking he was going to say a car, a million dollars, or something impossible, but he said, "I want s'mores!"

I said, "Okay, what do you really want?"

He said it again, so I asked, "Why s'mores?"

He said, "I've watched TV, and I see people around fires eating s'mores. They look so good, and everyone eating them looks like they're having fun."

I said, "Okay, you're getting s'mores and a campfire."

Picture this: an eleven-year-old sixty-pound boy sitting in his wheelchair by a campfire with s'mores all over his face. I never saw a kid happier. At the end of the weekend, I asked him what the most fun part of the weekend was for him after shooting bows and arrows, guns, seeing deer, and staying up all night playing video games. His answer was "s'mores!" Right then it hit me that something that cost less than five dollars changed this little boy's life. What he did not know was that he changed my life too. That little boy and thousands of children like him are my heroes! All of them born with disabilities that they had no choice over coming into this world, but they fight every day for life and to be accepted. If we could all stop and take ourselves back to being a child.

Remember running, playing, and pretty much doing anything you want, basically no worries in life. Well, special children want to do the same things, but their physical disabilities as well as social abilities hold them back. Society looks at disability as a reason to feel sorry for them and think, *At least, it's not me,* but you can learn so much from special children. They're full of ideas and love that is pure and no hidden emotion.

This chapter of my life began one summer while working with special children before I was injured. I got to see the daily lives of children and what it takes just to wake up, shower, and enjoy a day of life. I've always loved helping other people. I just never knew how special kids were until that summer. I saw their happiness and joy for life. These special kids loved everything they got to do. I knew then that one day I wanted to get these special kids outdoors enjoying all of the things I loved growing up like fishing, hunting, sports, and gardening.

So many times in life, we take for granted the things we enjoy, not realizing how many more others could love it too if given a chance. This is why I started OFF (Outdoor Friends Forever) after my injury and college. I wanted to get special kids the chance to enjoy the outdoors no matter their limitations. I came up with the name one day, thinking about the many memories I've had outdoors. I realized that most everyone I've met while enjoying the outdoors have become my friends forever. So the name Outdoor Friends Forever was born. We've been getting kids outdoors for many years, and I say we because there are many volunteers that help make these children's dreams come true. I'm so thankful to all the wonderful people who has volunteered and helped these special kids enjoy the outdoors. OFF is a nonprofit organization where we pair special kids with people that have special talents, and they enjoy the outdoors together.

I know you're probably wondering what makes up a special kid. The world calls them children with special needs. One day, I was talking to God and realized that we all have special needs in life, but very few of us are truly special like these kids. Some of them are so special that less than 2 percent of kids in the world have their particular life-changing need, and really, every disabled child is like no other in the world, so they are special. To show us just how truly special they are, God only made a few with disabilities like Down syndrome, spina bifida, hypophosphotemic rickets, and Friedreich's ataxia. For this reason, I call them special kids, not children with special needs. We have had so many special activities and adventures together in the outdoors. I have watched God work through these kids and change the lives of so many adult volunteers while helping these special kids. Yet another reason to call them special kids. I've gotten to watch these kids and adults grow vegetables, catch fish, become members of sports teams, and hunt together.

One story that I heard from volunteers was about feeding deer while hunting with the kids. I always tell our hunting guides to let the kids do whatever they want to do during their hunt because it is their hunt. They do things like playing games on a phone, eating snacks, and looking through binoculars. On one hunt, a special kid wanted to feed deer Oreos. All hunters know deer do not like smells that are not from the woods. The volunteers remembered what they had been told about letting the kids do what they want, so they let the kid throw an Oreo cookie out the deer viewing-house window. To the surprise of everyone involved, a deer walked out, and the kid was able to harvest his first deer!

Another memory from OFF is taking a father and son fishing for the day. I was able to get the son his own fishing pole and tackle box and then teach him how to tie lures on his line and properly cast it into the water. It did not take long for him to catch his first fish then another and another. Before long, he had caught so many fish his dad asked if he could fish as well (he really did not like to fish all that much). I said sure then showed him how to use a fishing pole. Then it happened! His son started showing dad what to do, and dad followed instructions well enough he caught several nice fish. By the end of the day, father and son had a wonderful day enjoying the great outdoors and making special memories as father and son.

A few months passed, the father called to tell me what I had done. I asked, "What?" The father informed me that they have a pond in their neighborhood, and for years, they just drove past it. He informed they never stopped until they fished with me. Now they stop once a week to fish together as father and son. He also included him and his son had never had an activity they enjoyed doing together until they went fishing. He said that I had made it possible for them to have something to look forward to each week. That is what Outdoor Friends Forever was established for: to help special kids enjoy the great outdoors with their family and friends.

I must tell you about a very special young man named Braden. Braden came to a hunt with OFF and got to shoot his first deer. He and I got to know one another on this trip very well. There was something different about Braden. We thought alike; we liked the same things and to hear his story was very similar to mine. People kept counting him out, and he kept showing the world what he could do! He shared with me about situations where other kids were picking on him at school daily. The kids were calling him names and making fun of him. It had gotten to the point that Braden's life had got pretty tough. He once told me that becoming friends with me changed his life.

Talk about God's plan. God knew we needed one another therefore He orchestrated it! He once shared with me that if I could do what I was doing, he knew he could do anything he wanted to do. That changed my life because here I was looking at him the same way! I view him as a very special young man with a disease less than one percent of the world has, and he gets up every day with a smile on his face and positive attitude on life. He pushes himself to keep going even when it hurts so bad. Most people would lay down, give up, and die. See, we were meant to meet because I see the best in him, and he sees the best in me. I love that young man with all my heart. It is pretty special in life to meet someone that travels the same road you do and understands the tears you cry and the blood you bleed. That is a good thing God put us together.

We once went on a hunt together for a deer he named Snowman because it was a piebald deer which is a deer with white all over its body. Less than 2 percent of deer in the wild have this piebald feature. We hunted on opening weekend of youth hunting season and were able to harvest Snowman. We both high-fived and celebrated the harvest together. You see, most would think that was just two people hunting that a killed a deer. Not a big deal. But it was not just a deer. Piebald deer makeup only 2 percent of the deer population, and it was killed by a young man that has a disease that only affects less than 1 percent of the world's population... enjoyed by two people the world classifies as special needs. But all we know is to give 100 percent of our hearts in everything we do. There is no doubt in my mind God put this relationship together. We now travel to churches sharing our story. God sometimes tries to put together people the world cannot see what they have in common. So don't let what the world sees or thinks stop you from being friends with anyone. Braden is just one of the many lives that OFF has had an impact on and in turn has had a major impact on OFF and me personally.

Another person who has had a big impact on OFF is a young lady by the name of Christina. Christina was diagnosed with Friedreich's ataxia when she was six years old. According to her doctors, she was destined to be in a chair by the age of eight, but due to her drive, she never used a wheelchair until the age of thirteen. As she was learning more about her condition, the doctor informed her that one in fifty thousand children are diagnosed with it. Once she heard this, she simply laughed and said, "Well, I'm the lucky one!" That is the way she lives her life daily, smiling and laughing through the hard times.

OFF recently started a program called The Outdoor Dream Hunt. Each year, one special kid is chosen, and they get to choose anywhere they want to go hunt. Christina happened to be the first person selected to go on this hunt, and she chose one of the best places in the country to harvest a mature buck, Texas. When OFF brought her into the board meeting to tell her the news, she began laughing. Some of us understood, yet others were a little confused. That's when she informed us that she was trying to laugh so that she didn't cry! She went to Texas for four days, all expenses paid, with her family. I was able to tag along to see her enjoy her dream hunt.

After the trip, we reminisced over her experience. She spoke of how "it was a beautiful ranch with so many things to see and do." She couldn't speak highly enough of the food specifically the cinnamon rolls and the venison meat loaf. One thing she was taken aback by was the sheer size of the ranch. She claimed that the drive to the lodge from the entrance of the ranch was comparable to driving through her whole home town! This was her opinion of the lodge itself. "The lodge we stayed in had amazing places to relax after hunts. There was a campfire we sat by at night where we were able to hear everybody's hunting stories from the day." She was overjoyed at the fact that the guides did everything in their power to ensure that she enjoyed herself, whether it be harvesting a mature deer and a bobcat or simply riding in a jeep for the first time. The biggest thing she took away from the guides however was that they were determined that she knew she was capable of doing all the things people commonly would say is impossible for a person in a wheelchair. In her own words, "It was a whole lot of fun doing the impossible!" One of the most memorable things she experienced during the hunt was getting to meet the ranch owner's son who happened to have Down syndrome. She was almost at a loss for words when she spoke about all the fun she had just hanging out with him while we were there. That right there is a God thing; we had no idea the ranch owner had a special son. I asked her if this dream hunt was everything she had dreamed of. She looked me directly in the eyes with a smile on her face and a tear in her eye and said, "I didn't get what a normal hunter gets in Texas…I got so much more. It was even better than I could have ever dreamed! The state was beautiful; the ranch was amazing, and the family that owned the ranch was so accommodating." In that moment, I knew the Dream Hunt program had done exactly what it set out to do: to make a special person's dreams come true.

One day, as we sat talking, she explained to me exactly why she loves OFF so much. She informed me that she has always suffered from high anxiety, yet being at OFF makes that all go away. To her, OFF is "heaven on earth." She claimed that she feels so normal at OFF because there, there are no disabilities—only special people. When I asked if she felt as though she truly had made "outdoor friends forever," she said no. She said that to her personally, no one there was friends forever but rather "family forever!" Needless to say, I shed a few tears because you never know what something means to someone until you ask. So do not run from God's plan. Give your heart to people, and God will put people in your life that will be there when you need them.

Now let me tell you about my special Kristi and God's plan.

Soul Mate

One of the biggest blessings in my life came while working with the Outdoor Friends Forever kids; one of the parents said they had a friend I needed to meet. So I agreed and called her friend Kristi to find out we had a lot in common. Kristi and I agreed to go on a date, and it was on that date I met my soul mate. She was beautiful, funny, smart, pretty fun to hang out with, and I liked the way she looked in her camo leggings. It was clear to me during that first date she was the one. I proceeded to write her a note on her napkin that said I was going to marry her. I've always heard you know when you know. After only one date and a few hours, I knew. And *yes*, we did get married.

This chapter of my life is one I thought might never come, and I had become okay with it. I had dated a lot of girls over the years, but for some reason, things never worked out. I had a plan, but God had a different plan. See, He wanted me to lean on Him with everything I had and just have faith. When I stopped looking for the right girl, God walked her right into my life. Our love grew fast and strong. We had many talks about our future and our dreams. We both have always wanted a child in our dreams.

One day, I drove her to the hill where we now have our home. Back then, it was just trees.

I asked her, "Can you see that?"

She asked, "See what?"

I said, "Our child playing in our yard."

She said, "You see that?"

I said, "Yes. Remove the trees, and it's all there—a pretty house with a pretty yard, and our child playing."

We both prayed and felt like it was time to start a family. We both always wanted to have children, but meeting in our late thirties and several medical issues, they were not on our side. We were fighting an uphill battle getting pregnant. With a lot of prayers, we decided to try medical help with pregnancy. We attempted five times to get pregnant through IUI, and it was not successful. Yet again, God was testing our faith. We depleted our savings to attempt this process. We were told that there was one last option, IVF, but it was really expensive, and the chances weren't much better. Then we prayed more and both decided we needed to try one more time. We decided to sell all our timber on our land to give us the chance to try one more time for a baby. Even after cutting all of the timber, we were still a little short for what we needed. My dad's land connects to my land, and on the property line, there were a few trees that would help us reach our goal. We only needed a small amount to make our goal, so I went to him to discuss my plan. He was so excited to help and give me some trees so we could have this chance.

It sure is awesome to have two great godly parents that always did their best to help me get anything I needed. At this point in our life, we put all our faith in God and used everything we had and asked Him to do the rest. So with this money, we went for our last chance at trying to have a baby. After enduring all of the treatments, we were blessed with four embryos. Those embryos were tested, and we were left with only one prefect embryo to try. The day came to try the process, and I continued to pray and surrendered it all to God. We waited with faith for the results, and the phone call came confirming Mrs. Hardy was pregnant. To see the joy in her face and the happy tears in her eyes was one of the most special days in my life. I will never forget it! God took me to the edge of my faith, and once I gave all I had and could not do the rest without His help, He showed up. We decided to name our little one Timber Faith Hardy. Without all of our timber and all our faith in God, we would not have our little Hardy princess.

See, I think God tested us allowing us to do things on our own for us to only find out we needed to rely on Him to do everything and anything in our life.

A Third Back Surgery

Lastly, I would like to tell you about one of those tough chapters: my third time of going to the hospital for back surgery. I started having pain so bad I could only lay in my bed, and the only way to get it to stop was fall asleep. Think of pain so bad when you sat up, you felt like passing out. I would try so hard each day to live a normal life, but I just couldn't function with pain. I had to go see my spinal doctor, and they did an MRI and found my spinal cord was stuck. With the cord being stuck, it caused severe pain and high blood pressure that was causing autonomic dysreflexia. My doctor said I was in need of a spinal surgery ASAP but just as I was told that COVID-19 hit our country. Thus causing me to lay in my bed for a couple months of bed rest and the pain was so bad I had to go to the emergency room four times during this bed rest. Each time, more medications were being added, and we're praying for surgery to relieve the pain and pressure. After going close to three months in pain, it made each day a challenge just to survive. During the time down, my wife had our baby, and I had to miss that because I couldn't sit up more than a few minutes without pain. So I watched my child being born on FaceTime.

After a couple more weeks of pain, my state finally opened up from COVID-19 where I could get my surgery done. But first, I must first pass a COVID-19 test to be cleared to enter the hospital for surgery. Let me tell you, them running that rod way up your nose is no fun. It felt as if they touched my brain when they twisted the rod around for five seconds. I passed the test and had my surgery. I spent fifteen days in the hospital in recovery, unable to sleep with stinging pain all over my back and sweating all over my whole body. I would be freezing one minute and hot the next. Each day, I was reminded of the first time in this same hospital recovering from my first injury some twenty years ago. I got reminded of those cold operating rooms and rolling down those long hallways in a bed not knowing where you're going. I was even once rolled into a dark room and left for over an hour alone. Those moments are not fun when you don't know where you are and when someone is coming to get you. My bed was rolled into so hard once that it knocked a fire extinguisher off the wall. As you'd guess, my back hurt very bad from the hit. As if that wasn't enough, the same lady who was pushing me back to my room ran over the trash can entering the room. Yes, I'll say what you're thinking. This lady doesn't need to be pushing beds anymore. Then there were nurses everywhere sticking me every day for blood and pain so bad you want to just go to sleep so it would go away. You fall asleep, and they wake you up every few hours to get more blood or give you pills. Hospital life is no fun but neither is lying in bed in pain every day for months, so sometimes in life, you have no choice. You have to get medical help. I've spent close to one hundred days of my life in a hospital. But one bright spot is the last visit; my very best friends and best men in my wedding sat with me every day I was in the hospital. That's true friendship for them to drop their lives and come be with me. Tough chapters in life don't last, but tough people do. Think about all the tough times you've had over the years that you thought would never end, and they did. God always got you through.

Wheelchair Humor

Welcome to the funny side of life in a wheelchair. It would not be me if I did not add the humor of the moments that happen living life in a chair. You have no choice but to laugh. Some of these moments cannot be explained yet others you can picture happening, but you cannot do anything about them. I have learned to just laugh at those moments you cannot change what happened. Why get upset and mad, just laugh. Enjoy life and do not get upset over something you cannot control.

It Was the Runaway Wheelchair

I woke up one day feeling really bad. I was running a fever, sweating, and saw no choice but to get in my truck and head to the emergency room to be looked at. Most people with spinal cord injury suffer from AD or autonomic dysreflexia. This is your body sending warning signals as to something is wrong below your level of injury. AD is nothing to play around with, so I went to the hospital to get medical help. I got there and drove around and around the parking lot looking for a space to park. Eventually, a car pulled out of a space just above the emergency room on a small hill. I pulled in and parked. I placed my wheelchair outside my truck door to get into, but before I got into it, I needed something off my back seat. As I was reaching into my back seat, I bumped my chair, and it started to roll away from my truck. It hit my truck, scratched it, then the wheelchair took on a life of its own. I guess being parked on a hill gave the wheelchair enough momentum to build up speed and roll into eight different cars on its way down the hill. It hit each car at such an angle that it looked like a pinball machine bouncing from one car to the next. Oh, and the best part of this whole story is that the wheelchair hit the last car so perfectly that it turned the chair straight and ended up at the front door of the emergency room. It was just a few feet from the emergency room door. So imagine me sitting in my truck in severe pain, running a fever, and trying to figure out how in the world my chair got to the front door alone. I was looking down a hill at my wheelchair parked outside the place I needed to be. Thankfully, about that time, a man came out of the emergency room and saw the empty wheelchair and saw me waving, and then returned it to me. His first question was how in the world my chair got down there. I told him he would not believe me if I told him.

What is there to do at a moment like that? Nothing but laugh. Next story that comes to mind is the day…

I Lost and Bought my Wheelchair Back

A pretty yet very off moment! Would you believe that my wheelchair was sold? Yep. I had to buy my chair back from someone. It all started one day when some friends and I were going to get something to eat. We left my home and drove about fifteen minutes away for lunch. Once we got there, we realized my wheelchair was gone. My friends had thrown my wheelchair in the back of the truck for the ride to town. One of them left the tailgate down, and the wheelchair was blown out of the truck on the ride over without any of us knowing. We immediately left and drove back toward my house looking all along the roadsides in hopes to see it without seeing it on the road, so we turned around to go back and look again. That was when we saw my wheelchair. There were two ladies just off the side of the road having a yard sale, and they had my chair! I drove up to them and asked for my chair back. They said they had gone inside to get something, and when they came back, there was a wheelchair in their yard. They thought it was a blessing to find a chair in their yard, and they could sell it to help them make money. I then explained what happened, and they understood, but to be nice, I gave them some money for watching my chair.

How about that story for funny? Well, just hold on. There is more.

The Day My Wheelchair Rolled Over Me

How about the time my own chair ran over me? Yes, it did happen! I was at home getting ready to go out. I realized I had something in my truck I needed to finish getting ready. I live way out away from other houses, so I decided to roll quickly out to my truck, not dressed. Because I knew no one would see me. To this day, I do not know why I was in a hurry since no other houses were around. Well, anyway, I rolled out of the house onto my deck and down the ramp toward my truck. When I got to the bottom of the ramp, the front wheels on my chair stopped, and I went flying out the front of the chair onto a concrete sidewalk that hurt badly on landing! As I was figuring out what happened, my chair came rolling at me and ran over me while I was lying on the ground. So let's put the whole picture together: me unclothed, lying on a sidewalk with my chair on top of me. I guess when I fell, my momentum threw me forward, and my body pushed the chair back up the ramp giving this thing with four round wheels momentum to come back down the ramp right at me as it reached me, lying flat on the ground and wondering what happened. It ran over my body as I was bleeding from the concrete fall and bruised pretty bad. That taught me a tough lesson. Then to make things worse, my date came over later and broke up with me. I guess I was run over in more ways than one.

Here is another funny story.

The Kite Chair

I once went to some friends for a party and enjoyed a nice evening watching a football game and catching up with friends. Late that evening, I decided to go home, so I went to my truck. Where I had to hook my chair to my lift, it raised my chair from ground over into the back of my truck for me. Well, I closed my truck door and forgot to push the button to lift my chair into the back of the truck. Then I drove away. I drove about fifteen to twenty minutes down the highway with my chair flying in the wind like a kite until someone on the highway stopped me by waving at me and showing me the chair flying beside my truck. Who knows what kind of damage it could have done to my chair had it not been flying. Rolling with the truck fifty-five miles an hour could have torn the wheels off, and it had it a mailbox or another chair could have been the loss of my chair. What an embarrassing deal! It is amazing that the chair hung on to that lift at sixty miles per hour flying in the wind.

Again, I just had to laugh because I was the dummy who did not finish putting the chair completely in the truck.

The Flying ATV

Well, this story is about one of the times when I threw my chair in the back of an ATV and rode around my property. It's much easier sometimes to get around in a motorized ATV if I want to cover more land. But with a new way of getting around, there are also more challenges that come with that. Most of you just turn the ATV on and push the pedal and go. For me, I either have to use hand controls or find a stick or cane to push the pedals with. Well, this is where this story begins.

I once was riding around in an ATV and stopping to look at my land in different areas. On this certain adventure, I was using a stick to push the gas pedal and brake. I pulled over to stop and watch some people walking on my land. I then decided to drive down the road to sit in another place and watch. But what I did not know was, while I was sitting parked at the last spot, I had pushed the stick down on the gas pedal, and it had stuck to the floor. Yes, stuck to the floor! There was a metal-plated surface on the floor of the cart for extra grip, and the metal surface had large grooves in it to add extra grip. Well, here's where the story gets interesting. Imagine you're in your car, and you crank it, and the gas pedal is stuck to the floor! Well, that's me; I crank the ATV, and the gas pedal is stuck to the floor. It goes from off to high speed in seconds. *My* problem came in that I was parked next to a large pile of brush and limbs. When I say large pile, I mean large, over eight feet high. This ATV was going straight at the pile of brush wide open. The ATV climbed the brush and launched me about ten feet into the air. Then as everyone knows, what goes up must come down. I started down from flying in this ATV front end first and landed out in the woods. Then once the cart hit the ground, it leveled off and headed out through the woods wide open again. I was very scared, not knowing what to do with this ATV, going wide open out through the woods, hitting limbs and stumps, and bouncing me everywhere in the seat. Then it came to me what to do to stop the ATV: turn the key off and then the motor can't run. So I reached down, turned the key off, and the ATV rolled to a stop. That was one wild ride from sitting still to flying across the sky and through the woods, not knowing what to do to stop it. See, just the smallest things like using a stick can cause problems that I never planned for.

I hope you enjoyed a few funny stories involving my life in a wheelchair. Life in a wheelchair is not easy; it's not always a smooth ride, but there are things and times I just have to sit and laugh. Why be upset, get mad, and waste time? Enjoy life and every special moment God has blessed you with.

The Chapters to Come

I've experienced good and bad times along my journey. There have been both struggles and triumphs while navigating this world in a wheelchair, but one thing I'm sure of is that God has placed the right people in each chapter of my life in order to bless me and help me through. He has never left me without help or something to learn from in order to prepare me for the next chapter of life. Over the years, I have accomplished so many things that most people would never have expected. It's hard to imagine that I would one day become the first in my family to graduate from a major university or that I would start my own business.

I am a four-time state champion football coach, a former professional fisherman, and a selling artist. I have found my soul mate, had a baby girl, spoken in front of thousands of people, and done so much more. I look back now and recall that I accomplished all these things after I heard a doctor say that I might live or die in the emergency room shortly after my accident. I think everyone has an image in their mind of how they think their life will play out, but God always seems to have something even better than anyone can imagine already planned out. As I contemplate the chapters to come, I begin to wonder what God has next for me. Who knows what all I'll be able to do before this life is over, but I do know that God has already made his plan for my life, and I am content to follow that plan wherever it may take me.

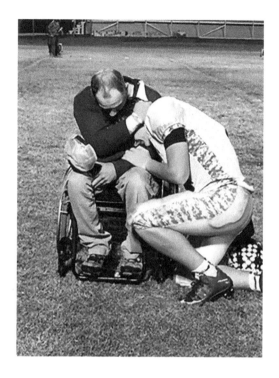

I hope that through my story, I have been able to show you a glimpse of my passion, love, and drive to enjoy life. I'm not a perfect person at all; I've made plenty of mistakes along the chapters of my life. God has taught me through them all. This life definitely threw me a curve ball when I went from walking to rolling but that has not deterred me. I figure if I am going to be thrown a curve, I might as well just hit that curve all the way out of the park and wheel myself around the bases of life. Many people may say that my chair makes it to where I cannot or should not be able to cruise on through all those bases, but that only fuels my drive to prove them wrong! It is abundantly clear that God has always had a plan for me—I think with my love to help others that He puts in my heart. Plus His plan had me work with special kids before my injury, and then after my injury, it was clear God allowed me to see from both sides. I have eyes from when I used to walk of how the world looks, and now I have eyes from a wheelchair. Maybe I'm the bridge to help some people to be able to see these special kids are truly special. We must all be mindful of the past we have come through only to see what He's brought you through, but we should also open our hearts to what God has in store for us in our future chapters of life. Never waste a moment of this life. Enjoy every day as if it were your last, and have faith in knowing that His plan is best.

If you are a caretaker, therapist, nurse, parent, or friend of a special person, remember this: there is always something that special person is capable of doing. I am no different than your special person. I simply had the courage to give some of the things in my heart my best effort, and most of those endeavors became great successes. Never hold a special person back. Instead, ensure they have every opportunity possible to do whatever it is they've always longed to do. Don't see the special need; see the special person for the way God made them just the way He wanted them. My favorite verse is Matthew 6:21, "For where your treasure is, there your heart will be also."

About the Author

Jim Hardy is an inspirational and motivational speaker. He has given his testimony hundreds of times in churches all over. He graduated from Auburn University with a degree in communications. Jim is currently enjoying traveling, speaking to high schools and colleges, and giving motivational talks on how to win every day. Jim can also be found relaxing in the outdoors with his wife, daughter, and their three dogs.